Wafiya

The Story of a Little Caterpillar

By Pascale Eenkema van Dijk
Illustrated by Michael Magpantay

Library For All Ltd.

Library For All is an Australian not for profit organisation with a mission to make knowledge accessible to all via an innovative digital library solution. Visit us at libraryforall.org

Wafiya: The Story of a Little Caterpillar

This edition published 2022

Published by Library For All Ltd
Email: info@libraryforall.org
URL: libraryforall.org

Library For All gratefully acknowledges the contributions of all who made previous editions of this book possible.

Original illustrations by Michael Magpantay

Wafiya: The Story of a Little Caterpillar
Eenkema van Dijk, Pascale
ISBN: 978-1-922835-14-7
SKU02709

Wafiya

The Story of a Little Caterpillar

Wafiya is a little caterpillar.
She is a few weeks old and is exploring
the world around her.

Wafiya walks over the branch of her tree and sees a big beautiful leaf and at the bottom of the leaf is a tiny round ball. *What is this?* wonders Wafiya.

She decides to ask her mum.

Mum explains, "Wafiya, that little ball is a tiny egg. Later, it will become a butterfly!"

"The mummy butterfly leaves hundreds of tiny eggs on leaves, and in each egg grows a little caterpillar just like you, Wafiya."

"So was I in an egg like that too, mummy?"
"Yes, Wafiya, that is how your life started."
At that moment, the little egg begins to move.
Wafiya is shocked!

A little caterpillar, much smaller than Wafiya, pokes his head out. He looks to the left and to the right. Wafiya is so excited!

The little caterpillar comes out, says a quick "hello" and then starts to eat. He first eats the little egg and then bites into the leaf.

He eats and eats and eats and eats.
His name is Maadhav. Maadhav and
Wafiya become friends.

While Maadhav is eating, Wafiya feels
that her skin is getting too small for her body.

This has happened before. Little caterpillars eat a lot and then they shed their skin to get a new skin, but this time something else happens.

Wafiya moves her body to the bottom
of a twig and attaches herself firmly
to the twig. She is going to shed her
caterpillar body for the last time...

Maadhav is watching as a shell forms around Wafiya's body.
Wafiya tries to wiggle free, but she is captured. The shell covers her entire body.

Maadhav is afraid and runs to Wafiya's mum. "Come and look, something is happening to Wafiya. I'm so afraid!"

Wafiya's mum and Madhaav return together to Wafiya, who is hidden in the shell. Mum is calm and explains to Madhaav, "Madhaav, you do not have to be afraid. Wafiya is growing up. She is a pupa now and she will come out as a butterfly with wings like me."

Madhaav is so suprised.

Then...
Wafiya breaks free, but Madhaav
hardly recognises her.

Wafiya is *so* beautiful. She has wings and can fly. Wafiya is very happy and now understands how the life of a butterfly unfolds.

Wafiya tells Madhaav everything about what happens with butterflies: how they start out as eggs, then become caterpillars, then pupa and eventually beautiful butterflies.

Madhaav is very excited. "So I will look like you one day?" She asks.
"Exactly, Madhaav, you will be equally beautiful."
Madhaav and Wafiya both smile and are very happy.

You can use these questions to talk about this book with your family, friends and teachers.

What did you learn from this book?

Describe this book in one word. Funny? Scary? Colourful? Interesting?

How did this book make you feel when you finished reading it?

What was your favourite part of this book?

download our reader app
getlibraryforall.org

About the contributors

Library For All works with authors and illustrators from around the world to develop diverse, relevant, high quality stories for young readers. Visit libraryforall.org for the latest news on writers' workshop events, submission guidelines and other creative opportunities.

Did you enjoy this book?

We have hundreds more expertly curated original stories to choose from.

We work in partnership with authors, educators, cultural advisors, governments and NGOs to bring the joy of reading to children everywhere.

Did you know?

We create global impact in these fields by embracing the United Nations Sustainable Development Goals.

www.ingramcontent.com/pod-product-compliance
Lightning Source LLC
Chambersburg PA
CBHW040313050426

42452CB00018B/2816